To:

_____

From:

_____

Date:

_____

Message:

_____

_____

_____

Just Enough LIGHT for the Step I'm On

BOOK OF PRAYERS

Stormie OMARTIAN

HARVEST HOUSE PUBLISHERS

EUGENE, OREGON

JUST ENOUGH LIGHT FOR THE STEP I'M ON BOOK OF PRAYERS
Copyright © 2002 by Stormie Omartian
Published by Harvest House Publishers
Eugene, Oregon 97402

ISBN 0-7369-1466-8

Printed in the United States of America.

05 06 07 08 09 10 11 12 / VP-KB / 10 9 8 7 6 5 4 3

Walking with Confidence Along the Path of Faith

I have discovered how handy it is to have special prayers to carry with me as I travel during the day, so that I will be reminded to pray about specific things. It's amazing how this simple act takes away the burden of trying to remember everything I need to pray about. And it keeps my mind free from being overloaded with concern about whether I have covered the issues of my life the way I should. That's why I am sharing the prayers in my book *Just Enough Light for the Step I'm On* with you. Plus I have added 21 new prayers as well.

Staying on the path to where God wants you to be is a walk of faith. And there is no greater comfort than knowing He is with you every step of the way. These prayers will help you to secure that kind of walk and give you peace in the process. They will remind you to cling to God as you step out of the past, live successfully in the present, and move into the future He has for you.

– Stormie Omartian –

Learning to Walk

Lord, I don't want to take one step without You. I reach up for Your hand and ask that You lead me in Your way. Thank You that no matter where I am right now, even if I have gotten way off course, in this moment as I put my hand in Yours, You will make a path from where I am to where I need to be. And You will lead me on it. I love that Your grace abounds to me in that way. Keep me on the path You have for me and take me where You want me to go. I commit this day to walking with You.

You will show me the path of life; in Your presence is fullness of joy; at Your right hand are pleasures forevermore.
— PSALM 16:11 —

Prayer Notes

_____

_____

_____

_____

_____

_____

_____

_____

_____

_____

_____

_____

_____

Learning to Walk

Lord, "cause me to know the way in which I should walk, for I lift up my soul to You" (Psalm 143:8). I know that when I try to run the race without You, I get off course. Thank You that even if I become weak and stumble, You will help me to rise again and continue on. And though I can't see exactly where I am going, I'm certain that You can and will enable me to get to where I need to be. Thank You, Lord, that You are teaching me how to walk in total dependence upon You, for I know therein lies my greatest blessing.

Come, and let us go up to the mountain of the LORD, to the house of the God of Jacob; He will teach us His ways, and we shall walk in His paths.
— MICAH 4:2 —

Prayer Notes

_____

_____

_____

_____

_____

_____

_____

_____

_____

_____

_____

_____

_____

Learning to Walk

Lord, I am committed to walking with You. Show me any place in my life where I have not taken the steps You want me to take. Help me to hear Your voice guiding me where I need to go. I surrender my life to You completely so that You can lead me on the path You have for me. I want to become more and more dependent upon You every day of my life. Help me to do that. I trust that Your ways are best, and I know that You always have my best interests in mind.

The steps of a good man are ordered by
the LORD, and He delights in his way.
– PSALM 37:23 –

Prayer Notes

_____

_____

_____

_____

_____

_____

_____

_____

_____

_____

_____

_____

_____

_____

_____

Beginning to See the Light

Lord, You are the light of my life. You illuminate my path, and I will follow wherever You lead. Protect me from being blinded by the light that confuses. Help me to always identify the counterfeit. I depend on You to lift up the light of Your countenance upon me (Psalm 4:6). Thank You, Lord, that because You never change, Your light is constant in my life no matter what is going on around me. Shine Your light through me as I walk with my hand in Yours. I give this day to You and trust that the light You give me is just the amount I need for the step I'm on.

The path of the just is like the shining sun,
that shines ever brighter unto the perfect day.
— PROVERBS 4:18 —

Prayer Notes

_____

_____

_____

_____

_____

_____

_____

_____

_____

_____

_____

_____

_____

_____

_____

_____

Beginning to See the Light

Lord, I pray that I will not be deceived and drawn toward the glittering light of the enemy. Help me to discern his deceptive tactics. Forgive me for the times I felt I was in the dark because I didn't recognize Your light in me. Help me to grow in faith so that I always trust You, the light of the world, to lead me through any dark times that come. May I never look to anything or anyone outside of You, Jesus, as a source of guiding light for my life.

This is the message which we have heard from Him and declare to you, that God is light and in Him is no darkness at all. If we say that we have fellowship with Him, and walk in darkness, we lie and do not practice the truth. But if we walk in the light as He is in the light, we have fellowship with one another, and the blood of Jesus Christ His Son cleanses us from all sin.

— 1 JOHN 1:5-7 —

Prayer Notes

_____

_____

_____

_____

_____

_____

_____

_____

Beginning to See the Light

*L*ord, I confess as sin any time in my life when I was going through a dark or difficult situation and I doubted You were there for me. Forgive me for that misunderstanding. I know now that You will never leave me nor forsake me. Help me to always trust Your Spirit in me to illuminate the path ahead as I walk on it with You. I acknowledge that You are the true Light who gives light to the world (John 1:9). Thank You that Your light will never be put out, and I can never really be in darkness when I look to You.

"While you have the light, believe in the light, that you may become sons of light." These things Jesus spoke, and departed, and was hidden from them.

– JOHN 12:36 –

Prayer Notes

_____

_____

_____

_____

_____

_____

_____

_____

_____

_____

_____

_____

_____

Refusing to Be Afraid of the Dark

Lord, thank You that because I walk with You I don't have to fear the dark. Even in the blackest night, You are there. In the darkest times, You have treasures for me. No matter what I am going through, Your presence and grace are my comfort and my light. Your Word says, "if one walks in the night, he stumbles, because the light is not in him" (John 11:9, 10). But I know Your light *is* in me. Jesus, You have come as a light into the world so that whoever believes in You should not abide in darkness (John 12:46).

Even the night shall be light about me;
indeed, the darkness shall not hide from
You, but the night shines as the day; the
darkness and the light are both alike to You.

– PSALM 139:11, 12 –

Prayer Notes

_____

_____

_____

_____

_____

_____

_____

_____

_____

_____

_____

_____

Refusing to Be Afraid of the Dark

*L*ord, I believe in You and know that You have lifted me out of the darkness of hopelessness, futility, and fear. I refuse to be afraid. I confess any time I have chosen to walk in the darkness of doubt, disobedience, or blaming You for my circumstances. Forgive me. I give my hand to You, Lord. Take hold of it and lead me. Thank You that as I take each step, the light You give me will be all I need.

Who walks in darkness and has no light?
Let him trust in the name of the
LORD and rely upon his God.
— ISAIAH 50:10 —

Prayer Notes

_____

_____

_____

_____

_____

_____

_____

_____

_____

_____

_____

_____

_____

_____

Refusing to Be Afraid of the Dark

Lord, I regard Your presence and my relationship with You as the most important thing in my life. Help me to never doubt it or take it for granted. In the times when You are testing my faith and my love for You, I pray that I will draw ever closer to You. Even in the most difficult situation of my life right now, I know that You are in control and will turn things around and bring good out of it. I refuse to allow fear or a lack of faith to keep me from walking victoriously in all You have for me.

For You will light my lamp; the Lord
my God will enlighten my darkness.
— PSALM 18:28 —

Prayer Notes

_____

_____

_____

_____

_____

_____

_____

_____

_____

_____

_____

_____

_____

_____

Embracing the Moment

Lord, You are everything to me. Thank You that I can walk each moment with You and not have to figure life out on my own. And when I come to a dark time, I can put my hand in Yours and depend on You as we walk through it together. I know that "the upright shall dwell in Your presence" (Psalm 140:13), and that's where I want to live. For in Your presence I will find healing, deliverance, love, peace, joy, and hope.

*For our light affliction, which is but for a moment,
is working for us a far more exceeding and eternal
weight of glory, while we do not look at the things
which are seen, but at the things which are not
seen. For the things which are seen are temporary,
but the things which are not seen are eternal.*
– 2 CORINTHIANS 4:17, 18 –

Prayer Notes

_____

_____

_____

_____

_____

_____

_____

_____

_____

_____

_____

Embracing the Moment

*L*ord, help me to embrace the moments of my life that are hard to get my arms around. Enable my eyes to see You in them. Help me to always acknowledge the abundance of Your goodness to me. I lift to You the deepest struggles in my life. I trust You to open my eyes to see all You have for me in them. Reveal to me the fullness of it all. Thank You that I can be filled with the joy of Your presence in every step I take, because You have given me the light I need for whatever step I am on.

In the day when I cried out, You answered me,
and made me bold with strength in my soul.
— PSALM 138:3 —

Prayer Notes

_____

_____

_____

_____

_____

_____

_____

_____

_____

_____

_____

_____

_____

_____

_____

_____

March 21 - 06

Embracing the Moment

Lord, help me to be content where I am right now on Your path for my life. I know You are always growing me into Your likeness and will not leave me where I am forever. I resolve to see any loneliness or lack of contentment in me as a sign that I need to spend more time with You. Help me to recognize Your blessings and goodness in the midst of every situation I face. Give me strength when I am weary and the fullness of Your joy when I feel sad. Help me to have an ever-increasing faith and a greater sense of Your presence in my life.

Though I walk in the midst of trouble,
You will revive me; You will stretch out
Your hand against the wrath of my enemies,
and Your right hand will save me.
— PSALM 138:7 —

Prayer Notes

_____

_____

_____

_____

_____

_____

_____

_____

_____

_____

_____

_____

_____

Dancing in the Footlights

Lord, shine the light of Your Word on the path of my life today. Make it a lamp for my feet so that I do not stumble. Bring it alive in my spirit so that it illuminates my mind and soul. Let it be a guide for every decision I make, every step I take. Keep me from turning to the right or the left so that I will stay on the narrow path that leads to life. Help me daily to carve out time to be alone with You and to feed on Your truth.

Great peace have those who love Your law,
and nothing causes them to stumble.
— PSALM 119:165 —

Prayer Notes

_____

_____

_____

_____

_____

_____

_____

_____

_____

_____

_____

_____

_____

_____

Dancing in the Footlights

Lord, "oh, how I love Your law! It is my meditation all the day" (Psalm 119:97). Open my eyes to see new treasure every time I read or hear it. Speak to me and comfort my heart. Make Your Word come alive in me and use it to nourish my soul and spirit like food does for my body. Align my heart with Yours and give me revelation and guidance so that I may know Your will for my life. Shine the lamp of truth where I am right now and show me the next step to take.

The entrance of Your words gives light;
it gives understanding to the simple.
— PSALM 119:130 —

Prayer Notes

_____
_____
_____
_____
_____
_____
_____
_____
_____
_____
_____
_____
_____
_____
_____
_____

Dancing in the Footlights

Lord, help me to spend more time in Your Word. Open my eyes to really see Your truth as I read it. Engrave it upon my soul so that it makes changes in me that last. As I read it, may it give me clarity, peace, security, and direction. Help me to remember to use Your Word as a weapon against the enemy of my soul. Fortify me with Your double-edged sword that is more powerful than any weapon the enemy would try to use against me. May Your Word bring light to any dark areas of my life.

For the word of God is living and powerful,
and sharper than any two-edged sword,
piercing even to the division of soul and spirit,
and of joints and marrow, and is a discerner
of the thoughts and intents of the heart.
– HEBREWS 4:12 –

Prayer Notes

_____

_____

_____

_____

_____

_____

_____

_____

_____

_____

_____

_____

Praying Your Light Bill

Lord, I thank You that You have given me all the light I need for this day. I want to experience everything You have for me, and I am willing to pay the price of obedience for it. So if there is any area in my life where I am not walking in full obedience to Your ways, show me. If You want me to do something that I am not doing, make me understand and enable me to accomplish it. Don't let me drift away. Pull me out of deep waters and rescue me from all that takes me from You. I lay down my will and surrender to Yours.

*Unto the upright there arises light
in the darkness; He is gracious, and
full of compassion, and righteous.*

— PSALM 112:4 —

Prayer Notes

_____

_____

_____

_____

_____

_____

_____

_____

_____

_____

_____

_____

_____

_____

Praying Your Light Bill

Lord, I turn away from selfish claims to my own life in order to heed Your direction. Take any rebellion in me and expose it with Your truth. "Search me, O God, and know my heart; try me, and know my anxieties; and see if there is any wicked way in me, and lead me in the way everlasting" (Psalm 139:23, 24). Lord, I choose this day to obey You because I know my life works best when I do. In the areas where obedience is hard for me, walk me through step by step. I don't want to do anything that would dim the light You have for my path.

For everyone practicing evil hates the light and does not come to the light, lest his deeds should be exposed. But he who does the truth comes to the light, that his deeds may be clearly seen, that they have been done in God.

— JOHN 3:20, 21 —

Prayer Notes

_____

_____

_____

_____

_____

_____

_____

_____

_____

_____

_____

Praying Your Light Bill

Lord, I thank You that You paid the price for my salvation. Help me now to pay the price of obedience for the fullness of Your presence in my life. Reveal any area of disobedience in me. Keep me aware of the subtle influences that can pull me away from the narrow path. Show me the things in my life that compete with You for my attention and attempt to get me off course. Enable me to clearly know the way You are leading me so that I am always in the right place at the right time.

*Enter by the narrow gate; for wide is
the gate and broad is the way that
leads to destruction, and there are many
who go in by it. Because narrow is the
gate and difficult is the way which leads
to life, and there are few who find it.*
– MATTHEW 7:13, 14 –

Prayer Notes

_____

_____

_____

_____

_____

_____

_____

_____

_____

_____

_____

Standing in the Line of Fire

*L*ord, I thank You for being my defender. You are more powerful than any plan the enemy has against me. Thank You that You will never leave or forsake me, and that You are always strong in my behalf. "I will lift up my eyes to the hills—from whence comes my help? My help comes from the Lord, who made heaven and earth" (Psalm 121:1, 2). No matter what happens, I will look to You to deliver me from the hand of all that opposes me.

Keep me as the apple of Your eye;
hide me under the shadow of Your wings,
from the wicked who oppresses me,
from my deadly enemies who surround me.
– PSALM 17:8, 9 –

Prayer Notes

_____

_____

_____

_____

_____

_____

_____

_____

_____

_____

_____

_____

_____

Standing in the Line of Fire

$\mathcal{L}$ord, I know that because I put my trust in You, You will be my shield (Proverbs 30:5). And I will not fear what man can do to me. "Lead me, O LORD, in Your righteousness because of my enemies; make Your way straight before my face" (Psalm 5:8). In myself I don't have what it takes to establish a formidable defense. I cannot protect myself and all I care about from the weapons of the enemy. But the enemy's strength is nothing to You.

Do not rejoice over me, my enemy;
when I fall, I will arise; when I sit in
darkness, the LORD *will be a light to me.*

– MICAH 7:8 –

Prayer Notes

_____

_____

_____

_____

_____

_____

_____

_____

_____

_____

_____

_____

_____

Standing in the Line of Fire

Lord, Your Word says that no weapon formed against me shall prosper (Isaiah 54:17). I know You have armed me with strength for the battle and will keep me safe (Psalm 18:39). Help me to "cast off the works of darkness, and...put on the armor of light" (Romans 13:12). Cause a song of deliverance to rise in my heart, and I will sing praise to Your glory as You fight the battle for me. I will walk with You through the enemy's attack, knowing that Your light on my path signals my certain victory.

Be strong in the Lord and in the power of His might. Put on the whole armor of God, that you may be able to stand against the wiles of the devil.
— EPHESIANS 6:10, 11 —

Prayer Notes

_____

_____

_____

_____

_____

_____

_____

_____

_____

_____

_____

_____

_____

_____

See What's Right with This Picture

Lord, I lay my worries before You and ask for Your mighty intervention to show me what's right when I can only see what's wrong. I am determined to see the good, so help me not to be blinded by my own fears, doubts, wants, and preconceived ideas. I ask You to reveal to me Your truth in every situation. Bless me with the ability to understand the bigger picture and to distinguish the valuable from the unimportant. When something seems to go wrong, help me not to jump to negative conclusions. Enable me to recognize the answers to my own prayers. I trust You to help me see the light in every situation.

And we know that all things work together
for good to those who love God, to those
who are the called according to His purpose.
– ROMANS 8:28 –

Prayer Notes

_____

_____

_____

_____

_____

_____

_____

_____

_____

_____

_____

_____

_____

See What's Right with This Picture

Lord, when I find myself in difficult or uncomfortable situations, show me Your perspective. Help me to see what's right and not all that appears to be wrong. Where I have failed to recognize Your hand of goodness and blessing in my circumstances, forgive me. Help me to make praise to You my first reaction to every event in my life. Deliver me from an ungrateful heart and help me not to complain when I should be giving thanks. I know You are a good God, and I trust You completely with my life. I rejoice in this day and every day because You are in charge of them all.

*I would have lost heart, unless I had
believed that I would see the goodness
of the LORD in the land of the living.*

— PSALM 27:13 —

Prayer Notes

_____

_____

_____

_____

_____

_____

_____

_____

_____

_____

_____

_____

_____

_____

Testing, One, Two, Three

Lord, grow me up in Your ways and lead me in Your will. Help me to become so strong in You that I will not waver or doubt. Make me to understand Your Word and Your directions to me. "Test me, O LORD, and try me, examine my heart and my mind; for your love is ever before me, and I walk continually in your truth" (Psalm 26:2, 3 NIV). I want to pass successfully through any time of testing You bring me to so that I might be refined.

You have tested my heart; You have
visited me in the night; You have tried
me and have found nothing; I have
purposed that my mouth shall not transgress.
— PSALM 17:3 —

Prayer Notes

_____

_____

_____

_____

_____

_____

_____

_____

_____

_____

_____

_____

_____

_____

Testing, One, Two, Three

Lord, I don't want to wander around in the wilderness, going over and over the same territory because I haven't learned the lesson. I pray that I will always have a teachable heart that recognizes Your hand in my life and soaks up Your instruction. Help me to trust Your timing. Establish in me an unwavering faith so I will know that when I walk with You, even the refining fire provides the perfect light for the step I'm on.

Praise our God, O peoples, let the sound
of his praise be heard; he has preserved our
lives and kept our feet from slipping. For you,
O God, tested us; you refined us like silver.
— PSALM 66:8-10 NIV —

Prayer Notes

_____

_____

_____

_____

_____

_____

_____

_____

_____

_____

_____

_____

_____

Testing, One, Two, Three

*L*ord, help me to count it all joy when I go through trials, because I know that when You test my faith it produces good things in me. I want to have the confidence and assurance that because of You, and all You have done and are doing in my life, I am complete and not lacking anything. Help me not to fail the tests of my obedience, faith, and love for You. I want to be perfected in those areas because I know it will be for my greatest blessings. I praise You in the midst of all that is happening in my life.

My brethren, count it all joy when you fall into various trials, knowing that the testing of your faith produces patience. But let patience have its perfect work, that you may be perfect and complete, lacking nothing.
– JAMES 1:2-4 –

Prayer Notes

Knowing How to Pack for the Wilderness

Lord, I am at home wherever You are. Shine Your light on the path You have for me to travel, for I know all my days are in Your hands. Forgive me when I grumble or have less than a grateful heart about where I am right now. I realize my attitude will have a direct bearing on whether I wander around in circles or whether I get through to the Promised Land You have for me. Help me to trust You for every step. Enable me to see all the blessings that are right here in this moment. I trust that Your grace is sufficient for this day, and each day that follows.

*My sheep hear my voice, and I
know them, and they follow Me.*
– JOHN 10:27 –

Prayer Notes

_____

_____

_____

_____

_____

_____

_____

_____

_____

_____

_____

_____

_____

_____

_____

_____

_____

Knowing How to
Pack for the Wilderness

*L*ord, if You call me into a wilderness experience, I will embrace it because I know that You will be there with me. Open my eyes to all the blessings You have for me in every moment of it. Whatever I need to lay down or forsake, help me to willingly and joyfully do so. I want to feel the solid ground at the center of Your perfect will. I don't want to grumble like the Israelites did and end up wandering around for years. I want to learn what You have to teach me so I can move on into all You have for me.

When He had called the people to Himself, with His disciples also, He said to them, "Whoever desires to come after Me, let him deny himself, and take up his cross, and follow Me."
– MARK 8:34 –

Prayer Notes

_____

_____

_____

_____

_____

_____

_____

_____

_____

_____

_____

_____

_____

Surrendering Your Dreams

*L*ord, I release all my hopes and dreams to You this day. If there is anything that I am longing for that is not to be a part of my life, I ask You to take away the desire for it so that what *should* be in my life will be released to me. I realize how dangerous it is to make idols of my dreams—to try and force my life to be what I have envisioned for myself. I lift up to you all that I desire, and I declare this day that I desire *You* more. I want the desires of my heart to line up with the desires of *Your* heart.

Delight yourself also in the LORD, and
He shall give you the desires of your heart.

— PSALM 37:4 —

Prayer Notes

_____

_____

_____

_____

_____

_____

_____

_____

_____

_____

_____

_____

_____

_____

_____

_____

_____

Surrendering Your Dreams

Lord, as hard as it is for me to let go of the hopes and dreams I have for my life, I lay them all at Your feet. I know that as I die to them, You will either bury them forever or resurrect them to life. I accept Your decision and fully submit to it. Lead me in Your path, Lord. I don't want to speak a vision of my own heart (Jeremiah 23:16). You never said life would be easy. You said You would be with me. I now take each step with the light of Your presence as my guide.

*I will rejoice in the L*ORD*, I will joy in the God of my salvation. The L*ORD *God is my strength; He will make my feet like deer's feet, and He will make me walk on my high hills.*

— HABAKKUK 3:18, 19 —

Prayer Notes

Surrendering Your Dreams

Lord, the greatest dream I have for my life and the deepest desire of my heart is (<u>name your greatest dream</u>). I surrender that dream into Your hands this day. Take the desire for it out of my mind and heart if it is not of You, and help me to die to it completely. If it is Your will for me, I trust You to resurrect my hope and make the dream happen in Your perfect timing. I give You all the gifts and talents You have put in me and ask that You would use them for Your glory. I rest in the joy and peace of knowing my life is in Your hands.

*Blessed be the LORD, because He has heard
the voice of my supplications! The LORD is my
strength and my shield; my heart trusted in
Him, and I am helped; therefore my heart greatly
rejoices, and with my song I will praise Him.*
— PSALM 28:6, 7 —

Prayer Notes

_____

_____

_____

_____

_____

_____

_____

_____

_____

_____

_____

_____

Waiting in the Wings

*L*ord, I wait upon You this day. I put my hope in Your Word and ask that You would fill me afresh with Your Holy Spirit and wash away all anxiety and doubt. I don't want my impatience or lack of trust to stand in the way of all You desire to do in me. I realize that even when my life seems to be standing still, as long as I cling to You I am moving forward on the path You have for me.

The LORD is good to those who wait for Him, to the soul who seeks Him. It is good that one should hope and wait quietly for the salvation of the LORD.
– LAMENTATIONS 3:25, 26 –

Prayer Notes

_____

_____

_____

_____

_____

_____

_____

_____

_____

_____

_____

_____

_____

_____

Waiting in the Wings

*L*ord, as I wait on You, help me to grow in my understanding of Your ways and not succumb to impatience or discouragement because my timetable does not coincide with Yours. Shine Your spotlight into any dark corner of my soul that needs to be exposed. Strengthen my faith to depend on Your perfect timing for my life. Help me to rest in You and be content with the step I'm on and the light You have given me.

I wait for the LORD, my soul waits, and in His
Word I do hope. My soul waits for the LORD
more than those who watch for the morning.
— PSALM 130:5, 6 —

Prayer Notes

_____

_____

_____

_____

_____

_____

_____

_____

_____

_____

_____

_____

_____

Waiting in the Wings

Lord, I choose to wait on You instead of just waiting for things to happen. I refuse to run ahead of Your perfect will for my life. At the same time, I don't want to lag behind it either because of steps I have neglected to take. Show me where I have not been diligent to do things You want me to do. I commit to trusting Your Word and delighting myself in You. I rest in You this day and wait patiently for You to bring to pass all that needs to happen in my life. Bless me with patience in the process.

Wait on the LORD; *be of good courage, and He shall*
strengthen your heart; wait, I say, on the LORD!
— PSALM 27:14 —

Prayer Notes

_____

_____

_____

_____

_____

_____

_____

_____

_____

_____

_____

_____

_____

_____

Expecting a Call

Lord, I know You have great purpose for me and a plan for my life. Open my ears to hear Your voice leading me into all You have for me. Align my heart with Yours and prepare me to understand where You would have me to go and what You would have me to do. Help me to hear Your call. If my expectations and plans are out of alignment with Your will for me, I surrender them to You. I let my desires for myself die. I would rather endure the suffering of that than the pain of never realizing what You made me to be.

You are a chosen generation, a royal priesthood,
a holy nation, His own special people, that you
may proclaim the praises of Him who called
you out of darkness into His marvelous light.
– 1 PETER 2:9 –

Prayer Notes

_____

_____

_____

_____

_____

_____

_____

_____

_____

_____

_____

_____

_____

Expecting a Call

Lord, because I want to hear Your voice say, "Well done, My good and faithful servant," when I meet You face to face, I will listen to Your voice now. I don't want to be unfruitful and unfulfilled because I never clearly heard Your call. I want You to fill me with Your greatness so that I may do great things for others as You have called me to do. I commit to walking this road step by step with You so that I may fully become all that You have made me to be.

Everyone who is called by My name,
whom I have created for My glory; I
have formed him, yes, I have made him.
— ISAIAH 43:7 —

Prayer Notes

_____

_____

_____

_____

_____

_____

_____

_____

_____

_____

_____

_____

_____

Expecting a Call

Lord, I know that Your call upon my life includes being a servant, obeying Your commandments, and always growing as a worshiper. Help me to do all of these things according to Your will. Show me where I am failing to do them as fully as You would like. I know I have been called out of darkness to proclaim Your praises. So I proclaim them this day and say all praise be to You, O Lord of heaven and earth.

Moreover whom He predestined, these He also called; whom He called, these He also justified; and whom He justified, these He also glorified.

— ROMANS 8:30 —

Prayer Notes

Believing It's Not Over Till It's Over

Lord, my times are in Your hands. Thank You that my life is never over here on this earth until You say it is. And when that time comes, I will see You face to face and dwell in Your presence. Thank You that You never give up on me, even when I have given up on myself. I am so happy that no matter what age I am, I will always have purpose because You have great things for me to do.

*Those who are planted in the house of
the LORD shall flourish in the courts
of our God. They shall still bear fruit in
old age; they shall be fresh and flourishing.*
– PSALM 92:13, 14 –

Prayer Notes

_____

_____

_____

_____

_____

_____

_____

_____

_____

_____

_____

_____

Believing It's Not Over Till It's Over

*L*ord, when it's time for me to do something different, help me not to cling to the past or be afraid to move into the future You have for me. Your Word says that Your plans for me are for good, and I know that I am secure as long as I walk through each day with You. Give me strength, courage, health, wisdom, revelation, and faith for the journey. I trust You to keep me on the right path and to continue giving me the light I need for the step I'm on.

Listen to counsel and receive instruction,
that you may be wise in your latter days.
— PROVERBS 19:20 —

Prayer Notes

_____

_____

_____

_____

_____

_____

_____

_____

_____

_____

_____

_____

_____

_____

_____

_____

Believing It's Not Over Till It's Over

*L*ord, I pray that You would give me an ever-renewing sense of Your purpose for my life. Use me for Your glory as long as I am on this earth. Help me to never be resistant to change, but instead to always be open to new things You want to do in my life. I don't want to hang on to the old life when You are wanting to make a new beginning. Help me to always be in Your Word, in close communication with You, and seeking only the counsel of godly people so that I will never miss Your light shining on the path You have for me.

Show me Your ways, O LORD; teach me Your paths.
Lead me in Your truth and teach me, for You are
the God of my salvation; on You I wait all the day.
– PSALM 25:4, 5 –

Prayer Notes

_____

_____

_____

_____

_____

_____

_____

_____

_____

_____

_____

_____

_____

_____

_____

_____

Surviving Disappointment

*L*ord, You alone are my guide, my companion, my strength, and my life. I need no other to fulfill my expectations, for all my hopes and expectations are in You. Show me what You want me to see. I refuse to allow disappointment to color my mind and emotions and outlook. I put You in charge of every detail of my life, even the pain I feel in my heart. Use it to perfect me and bring glory to You. Thank You for Your endless goodness toward me. I lift my hands to You, and I trust that the light I have is sufficient for what I face this day and this moment.

*They cried to you and were saved; in you
they trusted and were not disappointed.*

— PSALM 22:5 NIV —

Prayer Notes

_____

_____

_____

_____

_____

_____

_____

_____

_____

_____

_____

_____

_____

_____

_____

Surviving Disappointment

Lord, in times of great disappointment I will cling to You. As I walk through those times, teach me what You want me to learn. Reveal Your truth to me in every situation. Help me to see it clearly for what it really is. Keep me from fretting over my circumstances or living in unforgiveness regarding them. I want to, instead, wait in Your presence for You to reveal Your goodness to me in the situation. I want to always rest in You, knowing my life is in Your hands.

My soul, wait silently for God alone,
for my expectation is from Him.
— PSALM 62:5 —

Prayer Notes

_____

_____

_____

_____

_____

_____

_____

_____

_____

_____

_____

_____

_____

_____

Traveling Through the Dark Moments of Relationships

ℒord, I give all my relationships to You and ask that You be in charge of them. May Your spirit of unity reign in each one. If any are not of You, take them out of my life. Concerning my relationship with (_____), I ask that Your spirit of love and peace would reign between us. Lead him (her) in the way You would have him (her) to go. Bless him (her) and help him (her) to have a closer walk with You. Guide us both through any difficult times and help us to discern clearly the hand of the enemy when he comes to lie and destroy.

*If we walk in the light as He is in the light, we
have fellowship with one another, and the blood
of Jesus Christ His Son cleanses us from all sin.*

– 1 John 1:7 –

Prayer Notes

Traveling Through the Dark Moments of Relationships

*L*ord, shine Your light of revelation into every relationship I have and show me Your truth. Illuminate any darkness of unforgiveness in me, and I will confess it to You as sin. Bring reconciliation and clarity in place of misunderstanding. Where I need to humbly extend myself, enable me to make any necessary sacrifice and not cater to the cries of my flesh. Help me to lay down my life in prayer for my family, friends, and others You have put in my life. Teach me how to love the way that You do. I join my hand in Yours as I travel the path of relationships with Your unconditional love as my guiding light.

*Be kind to one another, tenderhearted, forgiving
one another, even as God in Christ forgave you.*
— EPHESIANS 4:31, 32 —

Prayer Notes

_____

_____

_____

_____

_____

_____

_____

_____

_____

_____

_____

_____

_____

_____

Traveling Through the Dark Moments of Relationships

Lord, I release all my relationships to You. Help me not to hold on to them too tightly, but instead to hold tightly to You. I know that the enemy wants to create strife and discord in my relationships, so I ask that You would be in charge of every one that I have. Help me to be humble, considerate, compassionate, and loving toward each person. Enable me to make the sacrifices I need to make for others as You reveal their needs to me. Help me to be unselfish as I look out for the interests of others.

*Let nothing be done through selfish ambition
or conceit, but in lowliness of mind let each
esteem others better than himself. Let each
of you look out not only for his own interests,
but also for the interests of others.*
— PHILIPPIANS 2:3, 4 —

Prayer Notes

Walking in the Midst of the Overwhelming

*L*ord, I can only make it through this time if I walk closely with You. While there are many things that can happen in life that are frightening or overwhelming, I know that Your power is greater than all of them. Even when what I experience is too much for me, it is never too much for You. Anything I face is nothing alongside Your ability to redeem it. Lord, I lift to You the things that frighten me most and ask that You would protect me and the people I love from them. Specifically, I bring before You (<u>name of overwhelming situation</u>) and ask that You would work Your redemption in it.

Hear my cry, O God; attend to my prayer.
From the end of the earth I will cry to
You, when my heart is overwhelmed; lead
me to the rock that is higher than I.

– PSALM 61:1, 2 –

Prayer Notes

_____

_____

_____

_____

_____

_____

_____

_____

_____

_____

_____

_____

_____

Walking in the Midst of the Overwhelming

Lord, I know that my enemy is the one who "has made me dwell in darkness…Therefore my spirit is overwhelmed within me…Cause me to know the way in which I should walk, for I lift up my soul to You" (Psalm 143:3, 4, 8). Whatever I need to do to make my path one of safety and peace, show me how and enable me to do it. Give me wisdom, strength, and clarity of mind to hear what You are saying to me in the midst of any dark or overwhelming situation. May my life be a testimony of the power of Your glory manifested as I walk in the light You have given me.

The LORD is my light and my salvation;
whom shall I fear? The LORD is the strength
of my life; of whom shall I be afraid?
— PSALM 27:1 —

Prayer Notes

_____

_____

_____

_____

_____

_____

_____

_____

_____

_____

_____

_____

_____

_____

_____

_____

Walking in the Midst of the Overwhelming

*L*ord, help me to recognize any fear in me as a call to prayer and a sign that I need to immediately draw close to You. Give me a clear sense of what is going on and show me how to pray about it. I know that Your perfect love will take away all my fear. Perfect me in Your love so that I don't fall victim to the torment that fear can bring. Give me a deeper sense of Your presence, for I know that Your presence is far greater than anything I might fear.

There is no fear in love; but perfect love casts out fear, because fear involves torment. But he who fears has not been made perfect in love.
– 1 John 4:18 –

Prayer Notes

_____

_____

_____

_____

_____

_____

_____

_____

_____

_____

_____

_____

_____

Reaching for God's Hand in Times of Loss

*L*ord, only You can fill that empty place in the canyon of sorrow that has been left in my heart. You are the one constant in my life that can never be lost to me. All else is temporary and changing. I know You are a good God and Your love for me is endless. Help me to cast my whole burden of grief on You and let You carry it. Even though there are times when it feels like I can't live through the pain, I know You will sustain me.

The people who walked in darkness have seen
a great light; those who dwelt in the land of the
shadow of death, upon them a light has shined.
— ISAIAH 9:2 —

Prayer Notes

Reaching for God's Hand in Times of Loss

*L*ord, enable me to get beyond any sorrow or grief I feel in my life. I realize life must go on, and I ask You to help me take the next step I need to take today. Even though it may be hard to imagine life without the pain I feel, with You all things are possible. Your healing power can restore anything—even a broken heart. Walk with me, Lord. I trust You to take my hand and lead me until I can feel Your light on my face and joy in my heart once again.

*Remember the word to Your servant, upon which
You have caused me to hope. This is my comfort in
my affliction, for Your word has given me life.*
— PSALM 119:49, 50 —

Prayer Notes

_____

_____

_____

_____

_____

_____

_____

_____

_____

_____

_____

_____

_____

Reaching for God's Hand in Times of Loss

*L*ord, where I have experienced loss in the past and still carry grief in my heart, I pray that You would take it away. I want to walk with You as You carry this burden for me. If I have not grieved properly, help me to cry every tear that needs to be shed in order for full release to come to my soul. If I have harbored any unforgiveness, bitterness, or resentment, I confess that as a sin before You and ask You to deliver me from these debilitating emotions. Thank You for Your comfort to me in my time of mourning.

Blessed are those who mourn,
for they shall be comforted.
– MATTHEW 5:4 –

Prayer Notes

_____

_____

_____

_____

_____

_____

_____

_____

_____

_____

_____

_____

_____

_____

_____

_____

Stepping Out of the Past

*L*ord, I release my past to You. I give You my bad memories and ask that You would heal me to complete wholeness so that they no longer hurt, torment, or control me. Bring me to the point where my past, even as recent as yesterday, will in no way negatively affect today. I give You my past failures in the area of (name any recurring problem). Set me free from this. Even though I may be unable to completely resist the pull of certain things on my own, I know You are able to set me free. Make me a testimony to the power of Your healing and deliverance.

*Therefore, if anyone is in Christ, he is
a new creation; old things have passed
away; behold, all things have become new.*
– 2 Corinthians 5:17 –

Prayer Notes

_____

_____

_____

_____

_____

_____

_____

_____

_____

_____

_____

_____

_____

_____

Stepping Out of the Past

*L*ord, I confess any unforgiveness in my heart for things that have happened in the past, and I release all persons who are associated with it. I specifically forgive (<u>name of person I need to forgive</u>). Lord, heal all misunderstandings or hurts that have happened between us. I know that I can never be free and healed if I tie myself to others by unforgiveness, so I ask You to bring to light any unforgiveness in me of which I'm not even aware. Give me Your revelation and show me all I need to see in order to walk out of the shadow of my past and into the light You have for me today.

Forget the former things; do not dwell in the past. See, I am doing a new thing! Now it springs up; do you not perceive it? I am making a way in the desert and streams in the wasteland.

— Isaiah 43:18, 19 NIV —

Prayer Notes

Stepping Out of the Past

$\mathcal{L}$ord, help me to be renewed in the spirit of my mind. Where I have made wrong choices in the past, I pray that You would forgive me and redeem those mistakes. Help me to forgive myself so that I don't keep replaying them in my thoughts. Take all of my past failures and use them for good today. I know that because I have put You in charge of my future, I don't have to fear that the events of my past will keep me from moving into all You have for me.

*That you put off, concerning your
former conduct, the old man which
grows corrupt according to the deceitful
lusts, and be renewed in the spirit of
your mind, and that you put on the
new man which was created according
to God, in true righteousness and holiness.*

— EPHESIANS 4:22-24 —

Prayer Notes

_____

_____

_____

_____

_____

_____

_____

_____

_____

_____

Maintaining a Passion for the Present

Lord, I want to live my life the way You want me to every day. Help me not to be stuck in my past, or so geared toward the future that I miss the richness of the present. Help me to experience the wealth in each moment. I don't desire to take a single step apart from Your presence. If You're not moving me, I'm staying here until I have a leading from You. I know I can only get to the future You have for me by walking one step at a time in Your will today.

This is the day the LORD has made;
we will rejoice and be glad in it.
– PSALM 118:24 –

Prayer Notes

_____

_____

_____

_____

_____

_____

_____

_____

_____

_____

_____

_____

_____

_____

_____

_____

Maintaining a Passion for the Present

Lord, I realize there is no better time than the present to be Your light extended to those around me. Help me to get beyond myself and become an open vessel through which Your light can shine. Give me Your wisdom and revelation, and show me all I need to see to keep me on the road You have for me. Enable me to step out of my past and keep an eye on the future by following Your light on my path today.

Let your light so shine before men,
that they may see your good works
and glorify your Father in heaven.
– MATTHEW 5:16 –

Prayer Notes

Maintaining a Passion
for the Present

*L*ord, I know that You have not made me to live in anxiety about anything. Thank You that, instead, I can bring my concerns to You and exchange them for Your peace which passes all understanding. Help me to never dwell on my suffering, for I know that it is nothing compared to the glory set before me when I walk through it with You. I reach out my hand to You this day so that I can walk safely in Your shadow.

For I consider that the sufferings of this present time are not worthy to be compared with the glory which shall be revealed in us.

— ROMANS 8:18 —

Prayer Notes

_____

_____

_____

_____

_____

_____

_____

_____

_____

_____

_____

_____

_____

Moving into Your Future

Lord, I ask You to be in charge of my future. I don't want to dream dreams if You are not in them. I don't want to make plans that You will not bless. I don't want to work hard trying to harvest something that will never bear fruit because I did not receive the seed from You. Help me not to waste valuable time getting off the path and having to come back to the same place again. I don't want to get to the end of my life and regret the time I spent not living for You.

Mark the blameless man, and observe the
upright; for the future of that man is peace.
— PSALM 37:37 —

Prayer Notes

_____
_____
_____
_____
_____
_____
_____
_____
_____
_____
_____
_____
_____
_____
_____
_____

Moving into Your Future

Lord, where I have made the mistake of doing what I want and then expecting You to bless it, forgive me. Instead I ask what You want me to do, knowing that when I do Your will, You will bless me. Enable me to hear Your voice and trust Your leading. I want it said of me when I leave this earth and go to be with You, that I walked with God. I want it said that Your glory was seen in my life. I trust my future to You, knowing You have it safely in Your hands.

*Arise, shine; for your light has come! And
the glory of the LORD is risen upon you. For
behold, the darkness shall cover the earth, and
deep darkness the people; but the LORD will arise
over you, and His glory will be seen upon you.*
— ISAIAH 60:1, 2 —

Prayer Notes

_____

_____

_____

_____

_____

_____

_____

_____

_____

_____

_____

Moving into Your Future

*L*ord, I surrender my past, present, and future to You now. Help me not to be anxious about my future but to rest in the knowledge that my future is secure in You. I want to keep one foot in eternity by never letting go of Your hand. I want to store up so many treasures in heaven that heaven will feel familiar the moment I arrive. And when I do take that final step into my eternal future with You, I trust that You will be there for me with all the light I need for that step, too.

There is surely a future hope for you,
and your hope will not be cut off.

— PROVERBS 23:18 NIV —

Prayer Notes

_____

_____

_____

_____

_____

_____

_____

_____

_____

_____

_____

_____

_____

_____

_____

Other Books
by Stormie Omartian

THE POWER OF A PRAYING® WOMAN
Stormie Omartian's bestselling books have helped hundreds of thousands of individuals pray more effectively for their spouses, their children, and their nation. Now she has written a book on a subject she knows intimately: being a praying woman. Stormie's deep knowledge of Scripture and candid examples from her own prayer life provide guidance for women who seek to trust God with deep longings and cover every area of life with prayer.

THE POWER OF A PRAYING® WIFE
Stormie shares how wives can develop a deeper relationship with their husbands by praying for them. With this practical advice on praying for specific areas, including decision making, fears, spiritual strength, and sexuality, women will discover the fulfilling marriage God intended.

THE POWER OF A PRAYING® HUSBAND
Building on the success of *The Power of a Praying® Wife,* Stormie offers this guide to help husbands pray more effectively for their wives. Each chapter features comments from well-known Christian men, biblical wisdom, and prayer ideas.

THE POWER OF A PRAYING® PARENT
This powerful book for parents offers 30 easy-to-read chapters that focus on specific areas of prayers for children. This personal, practical guide leads the way to enriched, strong prayer lives for both moms and dads.

THE POWER OF A PRAYING® NATION
Learn to intercede in practical ways for our political leaders, military personnel, teachers, and those who work in the media. Affect the strength and spiritual life of our nation through prayer.

THE POWER OF PRAYING™ TOGETHER (with Jack Hayford)
Stormie and her longtime pastor, Jack Hayford, look at the benefits and power of praying with others. More than just a "how to" book, *The Power of Praying™ Together* helps readers discover that when they are willing to link their hearts with others before God, they open themselves up to a wider, more interactive world of prayer.

THE PRAYER THAT CHANGES EVERYTHING™
Stormie shares personal stories, biblical truths, and practical guiding principles to reveal the wonders that take place when Christians offer praise in the middle of difficulties, sorrow, fear, and, yes, abundance and joy.

JUST ENOUGH LIGHT FOR THE STEP I'M ON
New Christians and those experiencing life changes or difficult times will appreciate Stormie's honesty, candor, and advice based on experience and the Word of God in this collection of devotional readings perfect for the pressures of today's world.